Dragonfly Migration

by Grace Hansen

ANIMAL MIGRATION

Abdo Kids Jumbo is an Imprint of Abdo Kids
abdobooks.com

abdobooks.com

Published by Abdo Kids, a division of ABDO, P.O. Box 398166, Minneapolis, Minnesota 55439. Copyright © 2021 by Abdo Consulting Group, Inc. International copyrights reserved in all countries. No part of this book may be reproduced in any form without written permission from the publisher. Abdo Kids Jumbo™ is a trademark and logo of Abdo Kids.

Printed in the United States of America, North Mankato, Minnesota.

052020

092020

THIS BOOK CONTAINS RECYCLED MATERIALS

Photo Credits: Alamy, iStock, Shutterstock

Production Contributors: Teddy Borth, Jennie Forsberg, Grace Hansen
Design Contributors: Dorothy Toth, Pakou Moua

Library of Congress Control Number: 2019956493
Publisher's Cataloging-in-Publication Data

Names: Hansen, Grace, author.

Title: Dragonfly migration / by Grace Hansen

Description: Minneapolis, Minnesota : Abdo Kids, 2021 | Series: Animal migration | Includes online resources and index.

Identifiers: ISBN 9781098202316 (lib. bdg.) | ISBN 9781098203290 (ebook) | ISBN 9781098203788 (Read-to-Me ebook)

Subjects: LCSH: Dragonflies--Juvenile literature. | Insects--Behavior--Juvenile literature. | Animal migration--Juvenile literature. | Animal migration--Climatic factors--Juvenile literature.

Classification: DDC 595.7052--dc23

Table of Contents

Dragonflies 4

Green Darner Migration 6

Globe Skimmer Migration. 14

Dragonfly Migration Route. 22

Glossary 23

Index 24

Abdo Kids Code. 24

Dragonflies

Dragonflies can be found all over the world. Some species travel great distances to lay eggs.

Green Darner Migration

Green darners of North America **migrate** each spring and fall. They can travel up to 900 miles (1,448 km). They migrate from Canada to the Gulf of Mexico.

It takes several **generations** to **migrate** this far. In early spring, the green darner leaves its winter home. It flies around 400 miles (644 km) north.

The group lands and lays eggs.

Then they die. The eggs hatch.

The young dragonflies continue

their journey north.

In September, the dragonflies fly south again. They also lay eggs and die. The cycle continues.

Globe Skimmer Migration

A more impressive migration happens on the other side of the world. The globe skimmer makes up to an 11,000-mile (18,000 km) journey. This is the farthest migration of any insect on Earth.

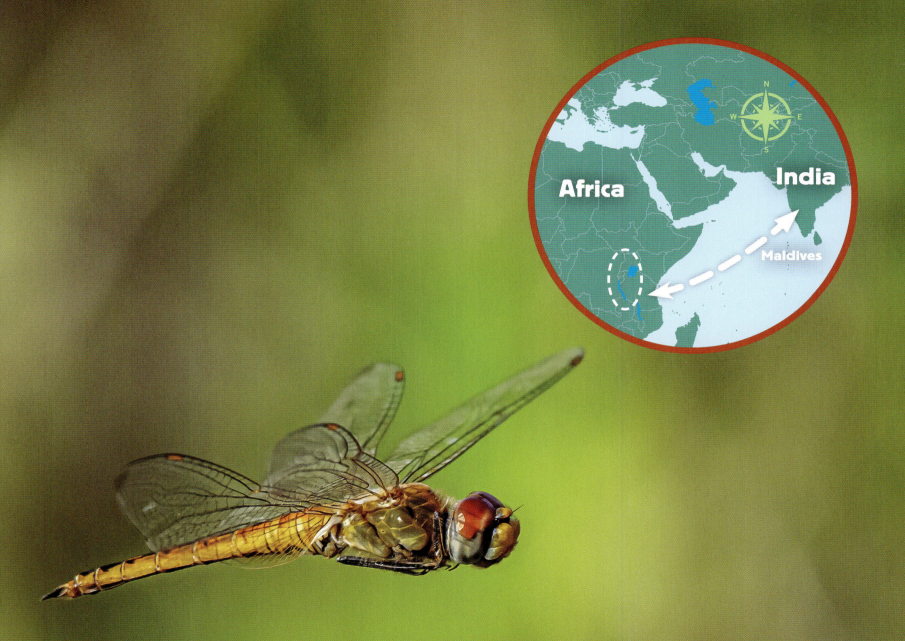

15

Globe skimmers of India follow the rainy weather that moves west. They do this because dragonflies need water to lay their eggs.

Many globe skimmers stop in the **Maldives** to lay eggs. Then they keep moving west across the Indian Ocean between July and December.

In time, the dragonflies will make it to Africa. Scientists believe the tiny insects are able to do this by riding the winds. They use their large wings to **glide** along.

Globe Skimmer Migration Route

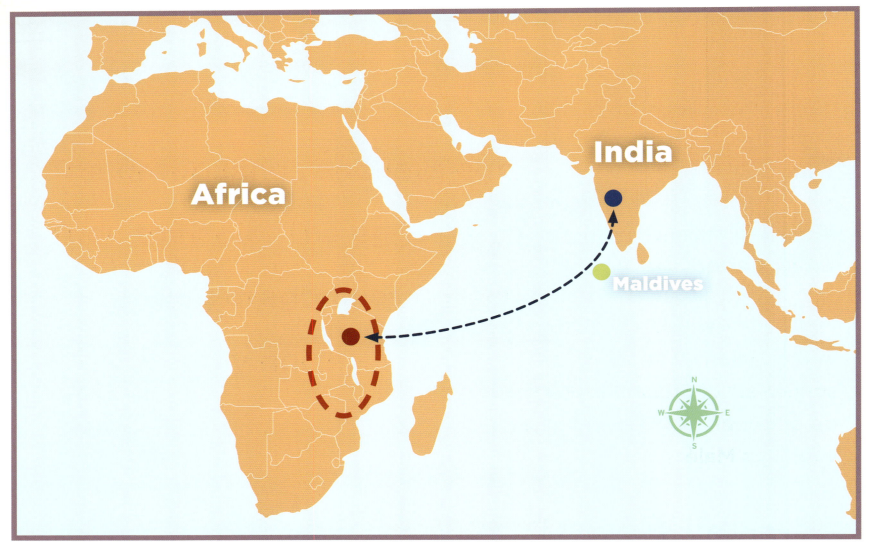

Glossary

generation – a group of living things that were born around the same time.

glide – to move smoothly and without effort.

Maldives – an island country in the Indian Ocean that lies southwest of Sri Lanka. It is made up of about 2,000 islands. Its capital is Malé.

migrate – to move from one place to another for food, weather, or other important reasons.

species – a group of living things that look very much alike and can have young with one another.

Index

Africa 20

climate 16

distance 6, 8, 14

eggs 4, 10, 12, 16, 18

fall 6, 12

globe skimmer 14, 16, 18

green darner 6, 8, 10

Gulf of Mexico 6

India 16

Indian Ocean 18

Maldives 18

North America 6

spring 6, 8

winter 8

Visit **abdokids.com** to access crafts, games, videos, and more!

Use Abdo Kids code **ADK2316** or scan this QR code!